# THE STORY OF
# JOHN F. KENNEDY

Written by Earl Schenck Miers
Editorial Production: Donald D. Wolf
Design and Layout by Margot L. Wolf

Edited under the supervision of
    Dr. Paul E. Blackwood, Washington, D. C.
Text and illustrations approved by
    Oakes A. White, Brooklyn Children's Museum, Brooklyn, New York

**WONDER BOOKS · NEW YORK**

# Introduction

John F. Kennedy had a special appeal to the youth of America. His outlook of optimism and courage was understood by young America, and indeed, by youth throughout the world. The spirit exemplified by President Kennedy was accepted not only by young people but by many older citizens as well, who saw in him and in his hopes for "the New Frontier" a challenge that gave vigor and purpose to America, and to other nations, in a time of transition.

*The Story of John F. Kennedy* tells a story that will in a few years become a legend. But in 1964, it recalls vividly events that are still a part of the living memory of all. For John F. Kennedy walks in our thoughts today even though his life and works are now history.

This is a time when we are struggling to guarantee that persons of all classes, creeds, and races may move into positions of economic and political leadership; to insure that the freedoms and rights of all responsible people are nurtured as national assets; and to give every individual a chance to achieve his fullest potential. These hopes, these goals were advanced immeasurably by the bold leadership of President Kennedy in guiding our nation toward greater political, economic, educational, and cultural opportunities.

*The Story of John F. Kennedy,* in relating his boyhood and youth, his schooling, his military and political service before becoming President, and his family life, makes clear why he can so aptly be described as "the first statesman of the Space Age, symbol of hope for securing peace in a troubled world, and the champion of equal rights for all citizens." It is a fitting memorial to the life and contributions of our recently martyred president.

*Paul E. Blackwood*

Dr. Blackwood is a professional employee in the U. S. Office of Education. This book was edited by him in his private capacity and no official support or endorsement by the Office of Education is intended or should be inferred.

# Contents

**Picture Credits:** Chief R. L. Knudson, the White House, Washington: p. 1.
Wide World Photos: pp. 2, 8, 9 bottom, 11, 12, 20, 21, 23, 24, 25, 29, 30, 31, 35, 36 top, 37, 38 top,
39, 40, 43, 44, 45, 47, 48.
Magnum: p. 16.
NASA: p. 41.
United Press International: pp. 4, 5, 6, 7, 9 top, 12 bottom, 13, 19, 36 bottom, 45.

Love Field. The fateful day of November 22, 1963. Texas Governor John Connally adjusts his tie (foreground) as President and Mrs. Kennedy settle into rear seats to prepare for motorcade into Dallas.

"John-John" salutes the passing casket on November 25, his third birthday.

The hushed procession that escorted the fallen leader's body from the White House to the Capitol on November 24 was one of the greatest ever seen in Washington.

*John F. Kennedy*

**What happened on a November day in 1963?**

On November 22, 1963, sun splashed down on Love Field, the airport in Dallas, Texas. Even as the big jet plane from Washington taxied to a landing, vast throngs broke into excited cheers. Then the plane's door opened and, bareheaded and smiling, John F. Kennedy, the 35th President of the United States, stepped into the warm morning light. Happily, he waved to the roaring crowds.

Kennedy, the youngest man ever to be elected to the highest office in the land, was then only 46 years of age. His youth, his confidence was, to many, like a kiss upon the cheek. Behind him, as he left the Presidential plane, came his younger and equally charming wife, Jacqueline Bouvier Kennedy. Next appeared Vice President and Mrs. Lyndon B. Johnson. At the Dallas airport, joy grew into delirium as the Presidential party came down the steps to shake the hand of John B. Connally, Governor of Texas. Red roses were heaped into the arms of Mrs. Kennedy.

White House advisors had warned President Kennedy not to make this trip to Texas, stressing the fact that when, in October, our United Nations Ambassador, Adlai E. Stevenson, had visited Dallas, he had been jostled by pickets and spat upon. There were in Dallas, these advisors warned, men violently opposed to Kennedy's policies.

But no President can isolate himself from any part of the American people, and here at Love Field, on that beautiful November morning, John F. Kennedy was glad to find so many friends. His face beamed at the raucous shouts. Gladly, he mixed with the crowd, shaking outstretched hands. In an open car, enabling him to wave to the people jammed along the roadside, he rode with Jacqueline in a motorcade bearing him toward the Trade Mart, where at noon he was scheduled to speak.

The motorcade moved on — the President saluting his admirers and Mrs. Kennedy, holding her red roses, radiant and smiling in the seat beside

him. At the corner of Elm and Houston Streets, in downtown Dallas, the limousine bearing President and Mrs. Kennedy turned sharply to the left. Here the road dipped toward an underpass. A police escort on motorcycles sped ahead.

Nearby stood a drab building known as the Texas School Book Depository. In a window, watching, waiting, with rifle raised, lurked a lonely man named Lee Harvey Oswald. Three times he pressed the trigger, wounding Governor Connally and killing President Kennedy.

A stunned nation, a shocked world, **How did the world react?** learned this news, at first unbelieving, then breaking into a grief unequalled since the tragic assassination of Abraham Lincoln.

Buddhist prayers in Tokyo, Japan.

The picture on page 6, and the photos below show some of the reactions of a shocked, grief-stricken world. Many foreign dignitaries came from all parts of the world to the President's funeral, among them Prince Philip of England, Prince Bernhard of the Netherlands, and King Baudouin of Belgium. At the graveside in Arlington, Va., stand President Macapagal of the Philippines, Emperor Haile Selassie of Ethiopia, and President Charles De Gaulle of France (front row right to left).

ica, a sobbing priest said: "Never again will we see his smiling face."

How, *why*, could anyone so young, a man who had served so short a time in the White House, so move the heart of all the world?

In Berlin, a torchlight parade of 25,000 mourners marched to the Court House, assembling in a square soon to be renamed John F. Kennedy Platz.

In London, among other signs of sorrow, the Union Jack flew at half-staff over Parliament.

In France, in Italy, in Spain, in every country around the world, people burst into tears at the news of the young President's death and hurried off to solemn church services.

In Rome, Pope Paul VI, filled with heartbreak, buried his head in his hands.

From every corner of the globe came messages of condolence and expressions of love for a young President whose life had been so needlessly wasted.

In New Ross, Ireland, whence the first Kennedy had left to come to Amer-

A torchlight parade in Berlin, Germany.

Flags fly at half-staff in London, England.

The Kennedys came to America, as

**Who were these
Boston Irishmen?** so many Irishmen did, because when in the late 1840's a blight ruined most of the potatoes in the Emerald Isle, one moved away or starved to death.

For $20 steerage, the Cunard Line carried a hungry Irishman from Cork or Liverpool to Noddle's Island in East Boston, and on this strip of warehouses, noisy stevedores, and illiterate immigrants, the first Pat Kennedy settled. On Noddle's Island, people lived in basements, fought rats, died of epidemics — it was not the happiest place to begin life in America.

How low could an Irishman fall? Wrote a good historian, and a sympathetic biographer of President Kennedy:

"The Irish were the lowest of the low, lower than the Germans or Scandinavians or Jews, or even the Negroes, who had come earlier and edged a bit up the economic ladder. Irishmen were lucky if they could find part-time work on the dock or in the ditch. . . ."

Pat Kennedy, like any other Irishman living on Noddle's Island at that time, did not care for anyone but an-

A farm near Dunganstown, Ireland, is the homestead of the Kennedy ancestors. The little stone hut on the left is the birthplace of Patrick Kennedy (pictured above), the President's great-grandfather. The President's cousins still live in the house next to it.

In June, 1963, the President visited Ireland and was warmly received by the Government, the people of Ireland, and the family which still lives there. Above, he visits with his cousins at the Kennedy homestead.

The kiss he gets from cousin Mary Ryan as a welcome brings a big smile to the face of the President.

At the request of the Irish Government, the Chief Herald of the Genealogical Office of Ireland prepared a grant of a coat of arms for President Kennedy. The presentation of this "O'KENNEDY COAT OF ARMS" was made at a ceremony held in the White House on St. Patrick's Day, 1961.

other Irishman. In this spirit, the Kennedy family began in America. They *had* to stand together.

Pat's last born son was Patrick J. Kennedy, who came howling into the world in January, 1862, or before the Civil War was a year old. That one day he might have a grandson who, like Abraham Lincoln, could become a martyred President of the United States, was the last thought to enter the head of an East Boston Irishman in those years.

Patrick J., like old Pat, was what Boston called "Shanty Irish"—the bottom of the ladder — but Pat J. had also that "go-ahead" streak which kids born in America took as their birthright. Pat J. began with a saloon, across from an East Boston shipyard, where other "Shanty Irishmen" gathered like flies around a sugar bun. Pat J., who rarely drank, let his patrons sing and become merry while he read books, usually about American history, and learned the tricks by which an Irishman forged ahead in politics.

To control one vote, in that age, was to show intelligence — control a hundred, and you practically ran your own political ward. Pat J., staying in the background and knowing this truth, learned the profession of politics so well that he rarely had to make a speech. The men working for him he called into a back room. They talked over what needed to be done to win an election. In the five years that Pat J. ran for state representative, he won every year. He won as state senator. He won any city commission job he wanted, for the Irish stuck together.

Another first generation Irishman in Boston in those years was John F. Fitzgerald, born in 1863 practically within the shadow of Old North Church, where during the American Revolution the lanterns had been hung to speed Paul Revere on his flight to warn the Massachusetts countryside that the British were coming.

Fitzgerald fought his way up as another "Shanty Irishman" — from custom house clerk to promising young politician. At the drop of a hat, "Honey Fitz," as he was known, would sing for anyone — and, without a drink, he would sing "Sweet Adeline."

No one ever expected "Honey Fitz" to have an opinion on any great national issue—"Honey Fitz" talked only of promoting a "Bigger, Better, Busier Boston," making him as effective a politician as East Boston would ever need.

So they were a queer pair, these grandfathers of the future President. On occasion, by luck, they might be friends — but more often, by choice, they were enemies. Each in his way forged ahead to a better life when, instead of being known as "Shanty Irish," they became "Lace Curtain Irish," or, as a jokester said, Irishmen who could afford to have fruit in the house even when someone was not ill.

Certainly neither of these old-time Boston political leaders ever expected, or wanted, their families to be joined. Pat's oldest boy, Joseph Patrick Kennedy, however, met Rose Fitzgerald and did not care how

**What made Papa different?**

John F. "Honey Fitz" Fitzgerald, President Kennedy's maternal grandfather and Mayor of Boston, in a typical pose.

Kennedy's grandmother (right) listens to Democrats make him their candidate. Until her death at 98, almost a year after his, the family shielded her from the facts of his passing.

much *his* father — or *her* father, old "Honey Fitz," now mayor of Boston — objected to their marriage. In 1914, Cardinal O'Connell married the dark-haired, rosy-cheeked girl to the son of the ward boss.

For Pat J. and old "Honey Fitz," the struggle from "Shanty Irish" to "Lace Curtain Irish" may have seemed the longest step in America, but their children already had made the step and saw no limit to where they now could go.

Young Joe, for example, born 1888, had sold candy and peanuts on Boston excursion boats at the age of nine, perhaps displaying the touch of the "Shanty Irish" that was willing to make a nickel anywhere. But afterward young Joe entered Boston Latin School, where he was both a good student and a fine athlete. Later he went to Harvard University, where, a member of the Class of 1912, he was at least a good average student.

Meanwhile Rose Fitzgerald, a quiet girl who had attended parochial and public schools in Boston and studied music in Europe, was by now far removed from the "Shanty Irish." After she married Joe, the children came in a steady line — Joe, Jr., born in 1915; then the future President, John Fitzgerald, born in 1917; then Rosemary, Kathleen, Eunice, Patricia, Robert F., born 1925, who was appointed Attorney General in his brother's Cabinet, Jean, and Edward M., born 1932, who in 1962 was elected to the U.S. Senate.

Making money became the first objective of Joseph P. Kennedy's life, and he made a lot of it. He made it in banking, in the silent movies, in whiskey, in real estate, in investments. No matter what he touched, he made money.

Mr. and Mrs. Joseph P. Kennedy posed with their nine children for this picture in 1938 at Bronxville, N. Y. Seated from left to right are Eunice, Jean, Edward (on lap of his father, Joseph P. Kennedy), Patricia, Kathleen; standing, Rosemary, Robert, John, Mrs. Kennedy, Joseph, Jr.

The house in Brookline, Massachusetts, where John F. Kennedy was born.

Joseph P. Kennedy was the father that John F. Kennedy, the 35th President of the United States, knew and loved. Jack could be comfortable in those early years — old Joe had already decided that young Joe, Jack's older brother, was to win the political honors for the family. The old man always got what he wanted: this was a family tradition.

**And what made Jack different?**

So John F. Kennedy was born 1917 in Brookline, a comfortable suburb of Boston where the "Lace Curtain Irish" then lived. Here, six blocks from home, he went to the Dexter School and was glad when old "Honey Fitz" stopped by and fetched him off to see the Red Sox play.

and 20¢ to lose. When I am a scout I have to buy canteens, haversacks, blankets, searchleigs [he never could spell], poncho things that will last for years and I can always use it while I can't use chocolate marshmallow sunday ice cream and so I put in my plea for a raise of thirty cents and pay my own way around. . . ."

Maybe Jack won, maybe he did not

Jack Kennedy in football uniform of Dexter School (about 1927).

Jack learned to swim 50 yards in 30 seconds.

But Papa Kennedy soon wanted to move from Boston's suburbs, and so, settling near the financial center where he operated, the family lived in the New York City suburbs of Riverdale and Bronxville. Jack attended nearby schools—he was "hot-tempered," teachers later said, causing his mother to visit the schools to discover why he was not doing better — and at about this time he addressed a petition to his busy father:

"My recent allowance is 40¢. This I used for aeroplanes and other playthings of childhood but now I am a scout and I put away my childish things. Before I would spend 20¢ of my 40¢ allowance and in five minutes I would have empty pockets and nothing to gain

— there is no proof either way. At 13, he was shuttled off to the Canterbury School in New Milford, Connecticut, where his letters home were filled with misspellings like "baggamon" for "backgammon," and "pacite" for "practice." He learned to swim 50 yards in 30 seconds, his best athletic accomplishment. He floundered miserably in

Latin. At Easter, an attack of appendicitis ended his stay at Canterbury.

The following fall, Jack was sent to the Choate Academy in Wallingford, Connecticut, also attended by his older brother Joe. Again, Jack was not an exceptional student, and teachers afterward described him as willing to coast along as a "gentleman C scholar," which meant that he did not too much care about Latin, French, English, and history as long as he did just well enough to pass these subjects. He was no better trying out for sports, never quite making any of half a dozen teams.

Jack's letters home proved that he knew he should be working harder. In his senior year, he wrote that he and his roommate, Les Billings, had "definitely decided to stop fooling around." Back came letters from Papa, who denied that he was "a nagger," but who said: "I definitely know that you have the goods and can go a long way. Now aren't you foolish not to get all out of what God has given you. . . ."

Jack doubtlessly believed that he was a fool — he graduated from Choate 64th in a class of 112. Surprisingly, classmates voted him the man "most likely to succeed."

Or perhaps this fact was not so surprising — with the Papa he had, with the older brother he had, how could Jack fail? The Kennedys now lived, among other places, in Hyannisport on Massachusett's Cape Cod and in Palm Beach, Florida. They traveled in Europe.

But Jack had his problems — not Papa, but *Joe,* who bossed the family behind the old man's back. Once, racing around the block on their bicycles, the two brothers collided. Joe escaped without a mark—Jack required 28 stitches.

Meanwhile, Papa, serving in President Franklin D. Roosevelt's Administration, moved on to higher posts until at last he was named Ambassador to England. If, sometimes, the Kennedys murmured that maybe one day Papa might become President of the United States, that whispering was not surprising. And if Papa did not make the Presidency, then brother Joe could — at least, such was Jack's impression.

Jack loved his family, for Papa had made loyal Kennedys of all of them. Tall and wiry when he graduated from Choate — a thin boy, really — Jack suddenly struck off on his own. Papa and Joe, Jr., had gone to Harvard — now, unexpectedly, Jack decided to enroll in Princeton. A summer in London, studying in the School of Economics run by the famous Socialist professor, Harold J. Laski, gave Jack a chance before college to meet all sorts of thinkers. Papa's guiding hand never wavered.

Illness plagued Jack all his life. No matter what he tried, sooner or later he was slowed down by one physical disability or another. In later years, a friend said that he learned to live so well with pain that only his eyes ever revealed his discomfort. In London, he was sick with jaundice, delaying, by several weeks after classes began, his entrance to Princeton. At Christmastime, he was sick with the same complaint — the year was lost.

**How did Jack escape feeling second-best?**

So in the end Jack, as a freshman, followed Papa and Joe, Jr. to Harvard. He had only one sport at which he excelled — swimming — and he stuck to it with tenacity. An agonizing time for Jack came when, trying to win his place on the swimming team for a meet against Yale, he was sent to the infirmary with grippe. He feared that the food the nurses brought would give him little strength for the competition ahead.

Really to know Jack Kennedy, one must touch his heart in this moment. All his life, he never had been anything but second-best in a family that wanted only winners. But Papa said all the time that coming in second did no good, which must have been difficult for Jack, flat on his back in the Harvard infirmary, wanting just once not to be second-best. He bribed his roommate to bring him steaks and chocolate malted milks — he would grow strong, he would win.

But Jack didn't win. Sneaking out of the infirmary, he swam with all his might for a place on the team, then returned to the infirmary as he had left — Jack Kennedy, second-best.

As a student at Harvard, Jack did even worse. A "B" in economics, a "C" in English, French, and history were the best he could do his freshman year — a far from distinguished record. His sophomore year brought him four "C's," a "D," and a "B," which were scarcely an improvement.

In Jack's junior year, he awoke — some say because his brother Joe had graduated. Perhaps rooming now with Torbert Macdonald, Harvard's great football star, helped to bring him into his own, but more likely the compelling influence was a trip he made to France, Spain, and Italy with his old friend from Choate, Les Billings, during the spring and summer of 1939.

Through Papa's influence, Jack met people no ordinary tourist ever saw, including the Pope, diplomats, the leading news correspondents. The letters and reports he wrote were sometimes wise, sometimes foolish — he was still a young man, forming ideas from a limited knowledge.

Jack returned to Harvard filled with a new enthusiasm, for, as his notes home revealed, he was not only doing better at his studies but also was "doing better with the gals." Stimulated by his travels in Europe, his thesis in his senior year was devoted to a study of why England had failed to recognize the rising menace of Hitler. This study won the approval of Jack's professors, who gave him a top mark, and from London a proud Papa cabled:

"TWO THINGS I ALWAYS KNEW ABOUT YOU ONE THAT YOU ARE SMART TWO THAT YOU ARE A SWELL GUY LOVE DAD."

For Jack, who so long had played second fiddle to brother Joe, this cablegram must have been a great reward. At last — for once — he was somebody as a Kennedy. Papa's influence not only encouraged Jack to rework his senior term paper into a book but also helped him to find a publisher.

Under the title of *Why England Slept*, Jack's first book became a national best seller. Papa's good friend, Arthur Krock of the *New York Times*,

15

The official Navy painting by Captain Gerard Richardson of the *Amagiri* ramming *PT 109* on August 2, 1943, in Blackett Strait in the South Pacific.

Lt. Kennedy in the Solomon Islands in 1943.

Part of the coconut shell with Lt. Kennedy's message.

At far right, Lt. Kennedy with members of the crew of the *PT 109* at a naval base in the South Pacific.

suggested the title. Another of Papa's good friends, Henry Luce of Time, Inc., wrote a laudatory introduction. The book appeared on the eve of when Nazi planes, roaring over England, laid this island-country in ruins — the timing was perfect for people to be interested in Jack's subject.

Jack's age — he was only 23 — led reviewers to treat the book with sympathy. Hard work, luck, good timing, Papa's influence — what better combination for success could a young man seek?

Afterward, however, Jack was at loose ends. He thought of attending Yale Law School, then switched to the business school at Stanford University. Six months study at Stanford was enough to convince him that he had yet to find his career, and so, still at loose ends, he visited South America.

As World War II spread over Europe to the Balkans and Russia during 1941, Jack could not deny his conviction that the rule of the Nazis was opposed "to law, to family life, even to religion itself." An old back injury, the result of his efforts to win a place on the college football team, led to Jack's rejection when he tried to enlist in the Army. For five months, he exercised to strengthen his back and won his reward when, finally, he was accepted by the Navy.

Jack's first assignments in Naval Intelligence, preparing a news digest for the Chief of Staff in Washington, then in working on plans to defend Southern defense plants against possible enemy bombing, hardly appealed to his active nature. Once more, Papa pulled strings and Jack went off to Newport, Rhode Island, and to Portsmouth, New Hampshire, for training in the handling of speedy little PT boats. His summers in Hyannisport had made him a natural sailor and Jack soon demonstrated an all-around skill at seamanship, engineering, and getting along with a crew. He was, instructors reported, "very willing and conscientious."

Meanwhile, in the South Pacific, the Allied forces began to push back the Japanese. In early 1943, Jack was in San Francisco, bound for war duty. By March, as Lieutenant (j.g.) John F. Kennedy, he commanded a PT boat in the action off the Solomon Islands. That summer, the Allies launched a vast air-sea-ground counterattack against the Japanese off New Georgia.

Jack, part of that counterattack, would never forget one date. Roughly, the time was a few minutes after midnight **What happened when the Amagiri struck?** on August 2, 1943. All day, American planes had been peppering the Japanese destroyer *Amagiri* and her commander, Kohei Hanami, was scarcely in a happy mood. In a night punctuated by squalls, the *Amagiri* plowed through the waters of Blackett Strait, west of New Georgia. Japanese gunners stood at their battle stations. They could sense the skipper's burning desire to strike back at a stubbornly cussed enemy.

In Blackett Strait that dark night, Jack Kennedy's PT boat ran on one engine in an effort to keep down her noise. At the same time, that single engine made the PT boat a sitting duck when, suddenly, the *Amagiri* loomed out of the night, churning the water at 30 knots. Jack's heart must have stopped momentarily — he had no chance as the destroyer sliced into the PT boat, amidships, like a meat cleaver cutting a leg of lamb in halves. Knocked down on the deck, Jack thought:

"This is how it feels to be killed."

Then he was in the water, very much alive. He began to take count. Two of his boys had been killed outright. A chap named McMahon had been badly burned when the engine caught fire, another named Harris had an injured leg. Jack led both back to the part of the PT boat still afloat. As daybreak came, they hoped for other PT boats to appear to rescue them. None came. So now what? Fight or surrender?

No one at Newport or Portsmouth had taught Jack what to do in a spot like this. But any fool could give up and drown. Jack now could thank God for all those hours he had spent on school swimming teams and sailing in the water at Hyannisport. A small island, three miles to the southeast, was their only hope for survival. He had been in the water almost 10 hours and it would take another five before, exhausted, he crawled onto the sandy strip of the island. He towed McMahon most of the way, holding the end of a strap in his teeth.

That night, Jack swam out alone to a reef, lugging the ship's lantern, on the chance of finding a PT boat. Once he saw the flash of a barracuda in the water, and knowing what these devils of the sea could do to a man, a shudder ran through his body. Cut and bleeding, he reached the reef and then swam on.

No PT boat appeared. Exhausted, he wavered between fits of consciousness and semi-consciousness as the current swept him in a circle. At last, he stumbled back onto the island beach.

Next morning, weak and sick, Jack led his men to another island. Thirst was their torture now, but when the men cracked open coconuts and drank the milk, they became violently ill. Later, when rain fell, they licked the moisture from leaves covered with bird-droppings, and they gave to the place the name of Bird Island.

A sailor who wore a rosary heard his friends say:

"McGuire, give that necklace a working-over."

McGuire grinned.

"I'll take care of all you fellows," he said.

And perhaps he did. With Ross, third officer, Jack swam to Nauru Island, nearer Ferguson Passage, where there was a greater prospect that a PT boat could be sighted. Here, they found friendly natives and Jack, using a coconut with a smooth shell, carved out a message:

"ELEVEN ALIVE NATIVE KNOWS POSIT[ION] AND REEFS NAURU ISLAND KENNEDY."

Taking the coconut, the friendly natives paddled off. For another night, in the high, choppy waters of Ferguson Passage, Jack and Ross searched for a PT boat. They lasted, at best, two hours.

But help was not far away — the natives returned with a letter from the commander of a New Zealand infantry patrol, telling them to follow the natives

At right, the "Temporary Citation" for bravery for Lt. Kennedy, signed by Admiral Halsey. Below, Lt. Kennedy is congratulated by Captain F. L. Conklin after being decorated with the Navy and Marine Corps Medal for his gallantry.

### SOUTH PACIFIC FORCE
OF THE UNITED STATES PACIFIC FLEET
HEADQUARTERS OF THE COMMANDER

In the name of the President of the United States, the Commander South Pacific Area and South Pacific Force takes pleasure in awarding the NAVY AND MARINE CORPS MEDAL to

LIEUTENANT JOHN FITZGERALD KENNEDY, UNITED STATES NAVAL RESERVE

for service as set forth in the following

CITATION:

"For heroism in the rescue of three men following the ramming and sinking of his motor torpedo boat while attempting a torpedo attack on a Japanese destroyer in the Solomon Islands area on the night of August 1-2, 1943. Lieutenant KENNEDY, Captain of the boat, directed the rescue of the crew and personally rescued three men, one of whom was seriously injured. During the following six days, he succeeded in getting his crew ashore, and after swimming many hours attempting to secure aid and food, finally effected the rescue of the men. His courage, endurance and excellent leadership contributed to the saving of several lives and was in keeping with the highest traditions of the United States Naval Service."

W. F. HALSEY,
Admiral, U. S. Navy.

to safety. The rescue of Jack, Ross, and all the men on Bird Island followed. They sang:

"Jesus loves me, this I know,
For the Bible tells me so . . ."

In that moment, crossing Ferguson Passage to safety with the crew singing "Jesus Loves Me," Jack Kennedy once again must have thanked God. They couldn't have lasted much longer — McMahon's burns had begun to rot and Ross's arm was hideously swollen.

**What made Jack "the poor little rich kid"?**

Jack, contracting malaria, fell to a weight of 125 pounds. The old back injury troubled him once more. Shipped back to the United States, he served for a time teaching the operation of PT boats in Miami. In the late spring of 1944, still ill, he was sent to Chelsea Naval Hospital, near Boston.

Tragic news awaited Jack, all the Kennedys. On August 2, 1944 — ironically, the anniversary of that night when in Blackett Sound the Japanese destroyer *Amagiri* had cut Jack's boat in halves — the family learned that Jack's older brother, Joe, was missing in a plane flight over German submarine pens along the Belgian coast. An explosion in mid-air had wiped out Joe's life. Jack read the news, saw his brother's picture on the front page of Boston newspapers, and rolled over, pressing his face hard against the pillow.

Lt. Joseph Kennedy, Jr., Jack Kennedy's older brother, who was killed in the war in 1944.

So, for the Kennedys, a series of tragedies began. Jack's sister Kathleen — his beloved "Kick" — was killed in an airplane crash in France four years later. Another sister, Rosemary, born with a handicap, lived in a nursing home in Wisconsin.

After an operation on his back, Jack left the Chelsea Naval Hospital and returned to civilian life in 1945. Thus, as the war ended, he found himself in the precise situation he had known when the war began — he was at loose ends. For the *New York Journal-American* and other Hearst newspapers, Jack went to San Francisco to report "from a GI viewpoint" the organizational meetings of the United Nations.

Papa decided — or so a Kennedy legend insists — that Jack was to take over for brother Joe and make a career of politics. That Jack accepted this decision with reluctance also is part of the family's legend.

For a Democrat to win the nomination in a primary in Boston's 11th District was the equivalent of winning election, and Jack picked this spot to make his bid for a seat in the United States Congress. The district, wrote one historian, was "a patchwork of some of the ugliest blighted areas in America. Irish, Italians, and a score of other immigrant groups were packed into grimy red-brick tenements sandwiched between smoking factories, oil tanks, elevated railways, dumps, and freight yards."

But both of Jack's grandfathers had fought their ways upward in similar political surroundings. Indeed, old "Honey Fitz" still lived in the Bellevue, a hotel in the 11th District where Jack also established his residence.

For a real "dogfight," it is difficult to find the equal of a Boston primary. In this battle, for example, there were 10 candidates, including two named Joseph Russo. Name-calling was taken for granted and Jack was labeled "the poor little rich kid" who should have stayed at home.

But Jack was soon to teach more seasoned candidates the real art of politics. He started campaigning early, and that start helped. He built his own political organization from old friends at Choate and Harvard and in the Navy — young men, like himself, who enjoyed a good scrap (which was no wonder, since they were almost all Irish). Younger brother Bob, just out of the Navy, rolled up his sleeves and went to work.

The "poor little rich kid" soon had

his opponents groggy. Sure, Papa had a lot of money — a valuable political asset, when it came to buying advertising space — but more valuable was Jack's smile. And his war record. And his ability to mix in any crowd, shaking hands. And his trick of putting aside name-calling and talking simply about issues in which the people were interested — jobs, housing, low rents, and prices. He carried his campaign into the people's homes, bringing the coffee and buns, and even the cups and saucers, with him. He was a whiz.

The result should have surprised no one — Jack rolled up 22,183 votes, almost double the vote of his nearest rival. And old "Honey Fitz," tickled to death, not only danced an Irish jig but rendered a good offering of "Sweet Adeline."

**What job next?** Jack was 29 years of age when he reached Washington to begin his first of three terms as a Congressman. His youthful appearance led him, some said, to be mistaken for a page boy and an elevator operator, and one veteran Congressman insisted on calling him "laddie." He dressed sloppily and often romped with the youngsters on a playground near his home in Georgetown. He liked going out with girls — he enjoyed *that* a great deal.

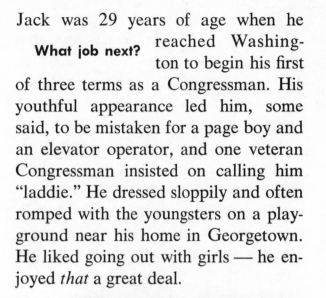

Left, Jack Kennedy, 29 years old, casts his vote with his grandparents, the Fitzgeralds, in the 1946 Primary in Boston, Massachusetts in which he is running as a Democratic candidate for Congress; above, during one of his campaign speeches, after winning the Primary.

21

And yet there was a serious side to Jack, especially on legislation that struck close to the interests of his 11th District — legislation concerned with wages, working conditions, social security, housing, prices, rents.

Once, arguing for a housing bill opposed by the American Legion, Jack shocked his colleagues in the House by blurting: "The leadership of the American Legion has not had a constructive thought for the benefit of this country since 1918!"

Other members of the House were quick to deny that they held any such critical view toward a veterans' organization claiming three million members. Jack romped back to his office, light-heartedly announcing to the staff that his political career was ended, but it was not. After all, it was the *leadership* of the Legion, not the Legion itself, that he had ridiculed.

Generally, Jack supported the policies of President Truman, although in the area of foreign relations there were sometimes distinct differences of opinion. After six years in the House, Jack knew that he could not be a Congressman forever. He wanted something more, but was not really sure of where he should turn in politics. Anyhow, in the House he was only *one* of 435 members — there *must* be something more important that he could do. He went back to Massachusetts to rebuild his political organization, not quite certain where, eventually, he would turn.

Jack talked to any group that would listen — in factories, schools, fishing clubs. He shook hundreds of thousands of hands. He drove himself relentlessly, eating bad meals on the run, reviving his old back injury so that every day he lived in pain.

By 1952, he had stumped almost all of Massachusetts' 351 cities and towns without knowing the position he was seeking. Should he run for a major state office or for the Senate of the United States? That April, by a peculiar twist of State politics — and the fact that, in the first place, Jack never wished to leave Washington — he announced:

"I, therefore, am opposing Henry Cabot Lodge, Jr., for the office of United States Senator from Massachusetts."

From the beginning, the campaign did not make too much sense. Lodge or Kennedy — where, really, was there much difference, except that one was a Republican supporting the Presidential nomination of Dwight D. Eisenhower and the other was a Democrat supporting Adlai E. Stevenson? Both were rich, handsome men. Both were loved in Massachusetts.

So the campaign, in the end, came down to a question of personalities — to "political know-how." Without opposition in the primary, Kennedy was required to submit nomination papers bearing 2,500 signatures. The chance was too good to miss — Jack put his organization to work and his nomination papers were filed with 262,324 signatures. Young Bobby Kennedy, the slave-driver for the family, was running the campaign.

And a great campaign it was. Both candidates had money — both candidates spent it. Both candidates had

On June 17, 1956, Jack received the Doctor of Law Hood at the Boston Garden from Dr. Carl S. Ell, President of the Northeastern University.

served in Washington, following almost identical ideas, and both candidates knew this fact. Thousands of copies of a *Reader's Digest* article, telling the story of Jack's heroism on his PT boat in World War II, were circulated in Massachusetts, but Lodge simply grinned — this was good politics, understandable politics.

The campaign for the Senate pleased Lodge at this point. Jack then did what, to Lodge, was almost "unforgivable" — he won. In Massachusetts, Eisenhower, running for President, beat Adlai Stevenson by more than 200,000 votes while Kennedy, a Democrat, beat Lodge by more than 70,000 votes. How, why?

The answer, really, was simple. Kennedy, fighting a personality vs. personality election, used his whole family to win. His mother, his sisters, came into Massachusetts to talk to other women about the election. Over the back fence — where there was a back fence in Boston — women told about hearing Jack talk and of having a cup of tea with his mother.

In a corner grocery store, at a morning's break over coffee, meeting a friend on the street, one heard the same name: "Kennedy, *Kennedy*." Papa's money could buy street signs, but no Kennedy money could purchase the political achievement of that moment when young Bobby, shy and fuzzy-haired as far as a razor was concerned, told an audience:

"My brother Jack couldn't be here, my mother couldn't be here, my sister Eunice couldn't be here, my sister Pat couldn't be here, my sister Jean couldn't be here, but if my brother Jack were here, he'd tell you Lodge has a very bad voting record. Thank you."

Who could beat this kind of political opposition? Lodge could not.

John F. Kennedy loved the United States Senate. **Who was the girl named Jacqueline?** Perhaps, when he first tried to board the subway from the Senate Office Building to the Capitol, a guard, asking him to stand back, added: "Let the Senators go first." If this incident occurred, Jack stood back — he never lacked for a sense of humor.

Yet the Jack Kennedy who reached the Senate was not the Jack Kennedy who had been elected to the House. Now he had beaten Lodge. Now he was somebody. The Senior Senator from Massachusetts, Leverett Saltonstall, offered his arm to lead Jack on January 3, 1953, to be sworn into office.

Jack had sense. As a young Senator from Massachusetts, he worked hard during his first two years to help the people who had elected him. He worked on bills for the fishing industry of Massachusetts, on bills helping its textile industry, on bills dealing with its ship-building industry, tariff protection for its watch industry, legislation protecting the Port of Boston and the Massachusetts transportation industry. On May 18, 1953, he gained the floor of the Senate to announce that for three days he would offer a series of speeches on New England's role in Federal Government.

Jack was now in love. When in 1951, he met Jacqueline Lee Bouvier, at a dinner party, she was then only 21. She was brilliant, gifted, beautiful. She had studied in France and at Vassar and now attended George Washington University in Washington.

Jack knew that he had met *his* girl, and in subsequent months he often would argue with the operator over nickels while trying to reach Jacqueline on the telephone. Sure he was in Massachusetts, politicking — what of it? Would Jacqueline meet him next Wednesday in Washington for a movie? Usually Jacqueline would — most of all, if she realized that the movie was a Western or a Civil War picture, which Jack especially liked.

Six months of hard campaigning for the Senate passed before Jacqueline heard from him. Working now as an inquiring photographer for the *Washington Times-Herald,* she learned a great deal about why men don't keep appointments and women wished they would.

For two years, the courtship between Jack and Jacqueline may have seemed hit-and-miss but on September 12, 1953, it ended in a good marriage. The Most Reverend Richard J. Cushing, then Archbishop of the Archdiocese of Boston, performed the ceremony.

Jacqueline quickly discovered that she had married into a family that made a mania out of sticking together. Touch football, the favorite sport of the Kennedys, played alike by males and females, became almost a matter of life or death. A visitor once described a game of touch football among members of the Kennedy clan:

". . . To be really popular, you must show raw guts. To show raw guts, fall on your face now and then. Smash into

Radiantly happy, John F. Kennedy and his bride Jacqueline leave church at Newport, R. I. on their wedding day.

The Kennedys cut their wedding cake while brother Robert offers encouragement.

Jacqueline soon became a valuable aide to her husband, shown here in his office in the Senate with his personal secretary, Mrs. Evelyn Lincoln (at left).

the house once in a while going for a pass. Laugh off a twisted ankle or a big hole torn in your best suit. They like this. It shows you take the game seriously as they do.

"But remember. Don't be too good. Let Jack run around you now and then. He's their boy. . . ."

Another passion of the Kennedys was "Monopoly," a game that they played to the point of exhaustion. Late at night, Jacqueline sometimes made a mistake, simply to end a game so that she could go to bed. Perhaps it was inevitable that sooner or later she and Papa Joe would clash. The moment occurred at Palm Beach, and the reason for the quarrel is now well forgotten. But Papa Joe, exerting his authority as chieftain of the clan, was suddenly interrupted by Jacqueline's flashing spirit. "You ought to write a series of grandfather stories for children," she reputedly said, "like 'The Duck with Moxie' and 'The Donkey Who Couldn't Fight His Way Out of a Telephone Booth.' "

For a moment Papa Joe sat, stunned. Then he burst into laughter, knowing that Jack had married the right girl.

Meanwhile, Jack had to live with his old illness, and during 1954-55 he was again hospitalized. Flat on his back, looking up at a hospital ceiling, he decided to write a new book. Pain — like money, like success — would be a recurring incident in Jack's life. But now Jack, gazing at his hospital ceiling, had to reach valid judgments. In *Profiles in Courage* he wrote a wonderful book, explaining what, to a Senator, the country must mean.

**Who were Jack's real heroes?**

Clearly, in his hospital bed, Jack was trying to answer those friends who told him, on first entering Congress, that "the way to get along is to go along." He gave his reply as "a man of conscience." He wrote:

". . . He [a Senator] cannot ignore the pressure groups, his constituents, his party, the comradeship of his colleagues, the needs of his family, his own pride in office, the necessity for compromise and the importance of remaining in office. He must judge for himself which path to choose, which step will most help or hinder the ideals to which he is committed. He realizes that once he begins to weigh each issue in terms of his chances for re-election, once he begins to compromise away his principle on one issue after another for fear that to do otherwise would halt his career and prevent future fights for principle, then he has lost the very freedom of conscience which justifies his continuance in office. But to decide at which point and on which issue he will risk his career is a difficult and soul-searching decision."

Jack Kennedy, looking up at the hospital ceiling, thought of the great men of the United States Senate who had made this decision — their lives became his *Profiles in Courage*.

The first was John Quincy Adams of Massachusetts, sixth President of the United States, who said: "The magistrate is the servant not . . . of the people, but of his God."

Another was Daniel Webster, a second Massachusetts man, who, in trying to save the nation from civil war, threw away his own political future.

In the same category, Jack placed Senator Thomas Hart Benton of Missouri and Sam Houston of Texas, both of whom, for unselfish reasons, tried to avoid an inevitable civil conflict.

Perhaps the finest chapter in *Profiles in Courage* tells the story of Edmund G. Ross, of Kansas, who, by a cussed streak of independence, prevented the impeachment of President Andrew Johnson. Senator Edmund Ross — like the other Republicans who supported him, making it possible for Johnson's impeachment trial to fail by a single vote — never again would be elected to office.

The case means nothing unless the facts are known. Abraham Lincoln, running for re-election, had asked a Tennessee Democrat, Andrew Johnson, to be his Vice-Presidential candidate. Obviously, Lincoln's choice had reflected a struggle within the House and Senate with his own party. Then the war ended — Lincoln was assassinated — and Andrew Johnson tried to carry on Lincoln's policies.

The conflict that followed ran deeper than the surface issues. Did the legislative branch of the Government have the right to destroy "checks and balances" within our system of government by ridding itself of an executive who opposed them by standing on his constitutional rights?

Upon this point, Andrew Johnson — the only President of the United States ever threatened with impeachment because he defied the legislative branch of the Government — was brought to trial.

Johnson won by the single vote of Edmund G. Ross of Kansas — American freedom won — and Jack's *Profiles in Courage* gloried in that fact. Later, he told the story of Lucius Quintus Cincinnatus Lamar, who tried to talk sense to his beloved home state of Mississippi after the Civil War, and of two in another period who were loved and hated — Senators George Norris and Robert A. Taft.

In his hospital room, Jack's mind ranged across the full scope of American history. He found heroes. No one can prove whether or not this fact helped him. Nor can anyone prove that it hurt him, either.

After a seven-month leave, Jack re-
**Why did the band play "The Tennessee Waltz"?** turned to the Senate on May 23, 1955. A basket of fruit on his desk, bearing the sign "Welcome Home," was a gift from the Vice President. When Jack reappeared on the floor of the Senate, the members stood in a body to applaud him, and Lyndon B. Johnson, then the Democratic leader, said simply: "We are glad to see you, Jack."

Kennedy had changed — Kennedy was a better legislator. With the help of veteran senators like Herbert Lehman of New York and Paul Douglas of Illinois, he fought a bill that by constitutional amendment would have changed the system of voting in the Electoral College to the advantage of the conservative elements — a bill, declared Jack, that really achieved nothing beyond the chance "to disrupt . . . thoroughly and . . . dangerously the American constitutional system."

Jack's fight helped to make him a national figure, but as a new Presidential election approached, the situation in Massachusetts became muddied. Jack favored the renomination of Adlai E. Stevenson, but to win control of the state's delegation required a bitter struggle. Jack won so well that friends talked of him as the natural running mate with Stevenson in 1956.

Papa Joe disliked the idea. He did not believe that Stevenson had a chance of defeating Eisenhower. He knew that Jack, as a Roman Catholic, must oppose an entrenched American prejudice against a Roman Catholic running for national office after the defeat of Alfred E. Smith (Catholic) by Herbert Hoover (Protestant) in 1928, and Papa Joe did not want to see this chance thrown away. Stevenson had lost once. He was a divorced man, thus making a great many happily married Americans skeptical of his ability to run a country if he could not run his personal life, and Papa Joe never missed an angle in evaluating a risk.

Jack, unlike his father, was willing to take the risk — he wanted the Vice-Presidential nomination, Stevenson, as the Presidential nominee, backed off, refusing to make a choice of running-mate between Jack and Senator Estes Kefauver of Tennessee. So the convention was asked to make the selection in little less than 12 hours.

A national political convention is an American invention. The frantic pace at which it usually operates becomes almost hysterical under circumstances like this. Sleep is forgotten. Aides dash off in dozens of directions, seeking to win the support of doubtful delegates. Other aides gather together the "hoopla" that is a convention tradition for every candidate — the placards, buttons, badges, noisemakers. In hotel rooms, pleas are made for the votes of states who are pledged to "favorite sons" on the first ballot, but who usually switch their votes thereafter. Meanwhile, the candidate frets over who will place his name in nomination, who will second him.

As the sleepless night wore on, Jack did not underestimate the formidable opponent he faced in Estes Kefauver. The first ballot was hectic, nerve-shattering, with Kefauver rolling up 483½ votes against Jack's 304, and the "favorite sons" trailing behind.

The second ballot — "the sweating-out time"— came now. Jack, toweling himself after a quick bath, stood before the TV set in his room as Lyndon B. Johnson gained the floor to announce that Texas had switched to Kennedy and "proudly casts its vote for the fighting sailor who wears the scars of battle." People in the gallery, clearly for Kennedy, rocked with cheers. The "switches" for Jack were piling up. When the second balloting was completed, Jack had pushed ahead of Kefauver, 618 to 551½ votes, and needed only another 68 votes to win.

Jack took nothing for granted. The TV screen pictured a convention bordering on pandemonium. Anything could happen. Now the Midwestern and Rocky Mountain States, remembering that Jack once had voted against farm supports they wanted, beat the band wagon for Kefauver. Everywhere, state delegations were waving their banners for recognition. Missouri gained the floor, announcing that it was switching its vote to Kefauver.

This was it — Jack had lost — and, finishing dressing, he rushed to the convention rostrum. There, young, handsome, calm, he moved that the nomination go to Kefauver by acclamation. The orchestra beat out "The Tennessee Waltz," making Kefauver's triumph complete.

And yet millions of TV viewers, watching the grace and smiling dignity with which Jack Kennedy had conceded defeat, would not soon forget this young man. Lincoln had lost to Douglas and become a national celebrity. In the same surprising way, Jack had won by losing.

**How did Jack win by losing?**

Suddenly, he was popular everywhere. Harvard gave him an honorary degree, citing his achievements as a "brave officer, able senator," who, "loyal to party," could still remain "steadfast to principle." After the convention, a trip to the Mediterranean was cut short by the tragic news that at Newport, where Jacqueline, expecting a baby, had remained with her family, an emergency operation had been required and the child had been lost. Jack rushed home. Their heartbreak was relieved in part when in late 1957 Jacqueline gave birth to a daughter, Caroline.

Meanwhile, Jack could not escape his role as a national figure. Every move he made in the Senate was watched now. Despite his youth, despite the fact that he was a Catholic, he *could* become a Presidential candidate. No matter what he did or said became a test of whether he had the ability to stand up against the eventual Republican candidate and against the rivals within his own party who also dreamed of winning the nomination.

No matter what was the issue — foreign affairs, civil rights, labor legislation — there was, in this political scuffle, both within and without Jack's party, a tendency to knock him down to size. His support of Algerian independence infuriated the Republican Secretary of State. He was called cowardly on civil rights for compromises that made possible gaining any bill at all in 1957. On labor, where he fought for internal reforms, he was opposed both by rivals within his own party and Richard M. Nixon, his future opponent, and managed to beat both by substantial margins.

Jack was swamped with invitations from all over the country to speak. Magazines wrote articles about him and sought articles from him on subjects as widely varied as foreign relations and "What My Illness Taught Me." In May, 1957, he won the Pulitzer Prize for

Jacqueline carries a "Stevenson for President" sign (at left) during the Democratic National Convention of 1956, where her husband, Senator Kennedy, is presented as "favorite son" candidate from Massachusetts for the office of Vice President.

Proud parents chat with Archbishop Cushing after he christened Caroline on December 13, 1957.

29

*Profiles in Courage.* Among the first six words that Caroline learned were "daddy, airplane, car"—clearly, "daddy," to Caroline, was somebody going somewhere.

To run for President, however, Jack had to remain in the Senate, and in 1958 he must stand for re-election. No one in Massachusetts believed that he had a chance of losing — that was not the point — but to remain a figure of national importance, a possibility as a Presidential candidate, he must win convincingly. Would all the time he and his staff had devoted to attending to every interest of Massachusetts, large or small, reap the reward he now needed?

Jack's opponent, an old foe from the Congressional contest of 1950, was Vincent J. Celeste, who greeted voters by saying: "I'm running against that millionaire, Jack Kennedy."

A typical Celeste statement ran:

"What right do Kennedy and his brother Bobby have to sit in judgment on labor without ever doing a day's work in their whole lives?"

And another:

"Look how my opponent [Jack] voted for the St. Lawrence Seaway — it starts right at the front door of the Merchandise Mart in Chicago, which is owned by old Joe Kennedy."

If Celeste believed Jack and Bobby never had done a day's work in their lives, both proved, in the 1958 campaign in Massachusetts, what it meant to work day and night. They were everywhere.

James MacGregor Burns, who wrote a fine biography of Kennedy during these years, remembered:

"The day before election, Kennedy campaigned for hours through factories and precincts in Boston. Finally, he and his party climbed wearily back into their car, sank into their seats, and started back to headquarters. The car stopped for an old woman plodding across the street.

" 'Stop the car,' Kennedy ordered. He climbed out, shook hands with the woman, asked for her vote, and climbed back in. . . ."

In 1944, Leverett Saltonstall had gone to the Senate with a plurality of 561,688 votes, the highest margin of victory in the history of Massachusetts. On that evening, when Jack stopped the car to shake hands with the old woman, Boston newspapers believed that he might do better.

Next day came the proof — Jack, with 1,362,925 votes, had beaten his opponent by 874,608 votes, a margin that broke all national records in such an election.

So Jack was on his way — where? Only one Senator in American history had ever made the jump directly to the White House, and he was scarcely

**Can another Senator win?**

During the 1960 Primary campaign in Maryland.

an inspiration for other hopefuls, since his name was Warren G. Harding.

But Jack did not despair — every poll said that his popularity was growing. His opponents among the Democrats aiming for the Presidency became a narrowing field of strong men—Adlai Stevenson, Senator Stuart Symington of Missouri, Senator Lyndon B. Johnson of Texas, and Senator Hubert Humphrey of Minnesota.

Jack ran hard. During the summer of 1959 he acquired a 40-passenger Convair plane, with a full crew, to carry him around the country. He went wherever he was asked, shook hands, made speeches, answered questions, appeared on television, gave interviews. Often Jacqueline accompanied him, complaining that her feet hurt. Meanwhile, campaign offices were opened in four rooms in the Esso Building near the Capitol, and the race for the nomination grew more feverish.

Jack was not the favorite candidate of the "pros" in the party and knew it. Lyndon B. Johnson, for example, was the choice of a fellow Texan, Sam Rayburn, doubtlessly the greatest Speaker of the House in American history. Behind Stuart Symington stood the solid support of a fellow Missourian, former President Harry Truman.

"Kennedy has nobody but his father and he does not always listen to him," one old party professional said. "He stays away from the bosses and the bosses don't like him."

The bosses had their reasons, believing everything was against Jack — his youth, his religion, his limited political background, his failure to stand as the champion of any one great issue in American life.

Jack knew the odds opposing him. He had learned something fighting for election to Congress from the 11th District. He had learned more beating first Lodge and then Celeste in running for the Senate. In losing the fight for the Vice-Presidency in 1956, perhaps he had learned the most — emotion as well as bosses ran a nominating convention.

Jack knew also that he must win in his own way, convincing the people, the politicians, the bosses by his performance in the primaries in such states as West Virginia, Wisconsin, Ohio, Oregon, California, and Nebraska. But Jack realized that he possessed assets — if he won, he would be the first

Senator Kennedy campaigning in Massachusetts.

Addressing the Convention after his 1960 nomination.

member of the World War II generation to reach the White House. He would stand for a new voice, a new hope in national politics and world affairs.

Jack made the primaries a shambles as far as his opponents were concerned.

**How do you become President?**

In Oregon, he disposed of that state's own favorite Senator, Wayne Morse, an example of political skill and power.

Senator Hubert Humphrey early recognized Jack's superior talents — organization, money, a tremendous human appeal — and yielded the field to Jack.

Lyndon Johnson was less inclined to withdraw, belittling Jack for months as too "immature" for the Presidency. The country's three leading Catholic governors — David L. Lawrence of Pennsylvania, Michael V. DiSalle of Ohio, and Edmund G. "Pat" Brown of California — were all reluctant to lend their support, believing that a Catholic could not win the Presidency.

In the first week of July, 1960, the delegates poured into Los Angeles for the National Democratic Convention. They numbered more than 4,500 and at least an equal number of newspaper reporters arrived to record what was decided.

The nerve center of the convention was the Biltmore Hotel, where Jack had his headquarters. Here, too, were the principal quarters of Johnson, Stevenson, Symington, and Governor Robert Meyner of New Jersey, all of whom were expected to play decisive roles in

the proceedings. The major TV networks likewise were headquartered at the Biltmore.

Jack brought to the convention a certain 600 pledged votes, meaning that he must pick up another 160 votes to win the nomination. Where were these votes to be found? Two farm states, Kansas and Iowa, backing their governors as "favorite son" candidates, represented 52 votes. Then there were five "unknown" states — Pennsylvania (81 votes), California (81 votes), New Jersey (41 votes), Minnesota (31 votes), and Illinois (69 votes) — that could swing the nomination.

Jack's "team," rolling into high gear, went after the doubtful votes. Nor did Jack fail in recognizing the fact that the opponent he must beat above all others was Adlai Stevenson.

The arrival of Stevenson in Los Angeles set off wild demonstrations. Thousands marched up to the Sports Arena,

32

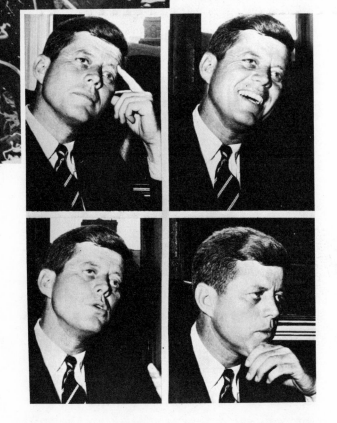

Left, on his final appearance in Los Angeles just before the national elections, the Democratic Presidential nominee is deluged with confetti and streamers; below, four typical expressions during a press conference in June, 1960.

where the convention was to be held, chanting: "We want Stevenson! We want Stevenson!" They carried a wide variety of placards: "ADLAI IS A MORAL MAN," "ADLAI IS A LOUSY GOLFER" (a slap at President Eisenhower, a good golf-player), and "NOTHING LESS THAN THE BEST — STEVENSON!"

The Stevenson "hoopla" was clearly the finest that Los Angeles would see, but conventions are governed by hard-headed politics. What was happening behind the scenes, among the doubtful

delegates, where the results really counted? The reaction in a few of the critical states reveals the type of "infighting" that goes on when the stakes involve nomination to the highest office in the land:

*New Jersey:* Here the influence of Papa Joe had been strong, winning support for Jack in the northern counties of the state, but Governor Meyner, resenting this challenge to his political leadership, refused to commit the state to any candidate.

*Minnesota:* Although released by Senator Humphrey from any pledge to himself, the delegates simply could not decide which way to turn.

*Pennsylvania:* Governor Lawrence, a staunch Stevenson man, allowed the delegates "to vote their conscience." Of 81 votes, 64 were for Kennedy.

*California:* The split here, coming late, would be even between Kennedy and Stevenson, excepting a few scattered votes.

*Illinois:* Here, for Stevenson, the result must be a matter of political life or death. A candidate without the backing of his home state had no hope. As the first Illinoisian to have a chance for the Presidency since Abraham Lincoln, Stevenson made his plea. But Papa Joe, with his large investments in Chicago real estate, had used his influence. Reluctantly, Stevenson had to be told the truth — Illinois was voting 59½ for Kennedy, only 2 for Stevenson — and long before the galleries burst into hysterical cheers as his name was placed into nomination, Stevenson knew that he was finished.

Thus the "infighting" went on, in

33

these states and elsewhere. Politics is like a battle — a ruthless game of tactics and strategy with only one winner. With Stevenson eliminated, the next opponent to defeat was Lyndon B. Johnson, and, no less vigorously, Jack's "team" set out to beat down the Johnson challenge.

How well the Kennedy forces devised their strategy and executed their battle plan was told by Theodore H. White, an observer of those moments as the convention cast its first ballot:

"At Illinois the candidate [Jack] was over the 100 [vote] mark. With Iowa, over the 200 mark; with his native Massachusetts, over the 300 mark; just short of 500 with New York; and over the 650 mark with Pennsylvania. In each case the morning tally of Room 8315 [Jack's room at the Bellevue] had been within two, three or four votes of actuality, and always conservative, as it was now developing. All along the way, as the Rocky Mountain states gave their vote, the Johnson tally was one vote, two votes, three votes, short of Johnson calculations. Earlier in the morning Bobby [Kennedy] had instructed the floor managers and shepherds to be ready at the call of the state of Washington on the roster; if at Washington in the alphabetical list the tally had passed 700, one could hope that with a little extra pressure 761 would be made before the alphabet was concluded. At Washington, the count read 710; West Virginia was sure now for 15 to make it 725, and Wisconsin with 23 to make it 748.

"The candidate leaned forward — Wyoming, on the next call, could make

it. On the floor Bobby and Teddy [now Senator Edward Kennedy] were equally alert, and the TV camera showed Teddy Kennedy deep among the Wyoming delegates, whom he had cultivated since the previous fall.

" 'This could make it,' said the candidate . . .

" 'Wyoming,' chanted Tracy S. Mc-Craken, Wyoming's national committeeman, 'casts all fifteen votes for the next President of the United States.' "

The total now was 763 — Jack was "in."

Jack's surprise selection of a running-mate was Lyndon Johnson. The Republican nominees were Richard M. Nixon, who had served two terms as Eisenhower's Vice President, and Henry Cabot Lodge, Jr., who had opposed Jack in the Massachusetts senatorial election eight years before.

**How did Jack win?**

A rigorous campaign followed. Jack faced up to the religious issue, telling a Texas audience: "I believe in an America where the separation of church and state is absolute . . . where no public official either requests or accepts instructions on public policy from . . . [an] ecclesiastical source." Jack's statement, Nixon said, should be accepted by the voters "without further questioning."

Meanwhile, the campaign reached the sizzling point as Jack kept pounding on the themes that under the Republicans the country was "losing prestige" abroad and "standing still" at home. A highlight of the campaign was a series of television debates between the Presi-

How the two candidates, Senator Kennedy, Democrat, and Vice President Richard M. Nixon, Republican, appeared to the viewers during their second debate on the air.

dential contenders and there could be little question but that Jack benefited from these appearances by seeming far from the youthful incompetent his opponent tried to label him.

Americans in record numbers turned out on Election Day to choose between Kennedy and Nixon and the result was decided by an eyewink. The popular vote for Nixon was 34,108,474, and for Kennedy, 34,221,531. In the Electoral College vote, the Democratic candidate won by a margin of 303 to 219.

Never more would the youthful statesman from Massachusetts be called "Jack," even by his closest friends — he was now John F. Kennedy, 35th President of the United States. Now he held the most powerful office in the world, and, as he would quickly learn, also the loneliest. Now he belonged to history.

## The Presidential Years

President Kennedy was inaugurated on January 20, 1961, a snowy day in Washington. His inaugural address called for a national dedication to a worldwide struggle against the forces of tyranny, poverty, disease, and war.

**Why did the country forgive his 1961 "mistake"?**

"Ask not what your country can do for you," he said. "Ask what you can do for your country." Young and handsome, he captured the hearts of the American people, who liked seeing this youthful man and his beautiful wife in the White House. They liked having young children there — pretty, blonde

35

John F. Kennedy, his left hand resting on an old family Bible, repeats after Chief Justice Warren the oath of office. Vice President Johnson stands behind the new President of the United States.

President Kennedy delivers his State of the Union Message to a joint session of Congress. Behind the President sit Vice President Johnson and Speaker of the House John McCormack.

Caroline and John Fitzgerald Kennedy Jr., who was born on November 25, 1960.

Quickly, pressures were placed on President Kennedy to test his strength, his wisdom, for the Communist bloc, under the leadership of Premier Nikita Khrushchev, intended to permit no breathing period in the cold war for world domination. February brought a crisis in the Congo, March a crisis in Laos — clearly, the young President was to be given little chance to grow into his job.

April brought a new crisis in Cuba, where the Communist-dominated Fidel Castro ruled. On April 15, America learned that three B-26 planes, armed by anti-Castro forces, had bombed the island's military airports, and next day it was reported that troops opposed to Castro and trained in the United States had invaded Cuba's Oriente province. Actually, the invasion had occurred elsewhere — in the Bay of Cochinos or "Bay of Pigs."

About 1,500 men were involved in the landings. With little ammunition and no air support, their early success, apparently, arose from the fact that several battalions of Castro's militiamen were willing to aid them.

Then the strength of Castro's tanks and airplanes turned the tide against the luckless invaders. Our nation's Central Intelligence Agency was blamed for poor advice in planning the invasion. Castro, as the spearhead of Communist penetration into the Western Hemisphere with a base only 90 miles off the southern tip of the American mainland, seemed stronger than ever.

President Kennedy accepted "full responsibility" for the failure at the Bay of Pigs, and the country responded warmly. On television, people watched this young man facing the nation's best reporters and answering their questions openly and with knowledge. His popularity grew. The people had a sense of sharing in the toughest job on earth and tried to grow with the thoughtful man who was their elected leader.

The pressures did not cease. June brought a new emergency in Berlin, leading to the building of the Berlin Wall. Kennedy stood firm, calling for vast increases in defense spending to oppose this threat of Communist aggression and Congress, like the people, supported the young President until, slowly but clearly, the Communists began to back down as though taking a second look at John F. Kennedy and realizing that there was real backbone in this fellow.

Fall brought another crisis in South Vietnam, however. Nuclear testing in the air was resumed by the Soviets. Kennedy, growing with his responsibilities, made a trip to Puerto Rico, Venezuela, and Colombia, announcing his "Alliance for Progress," a program by which Latin-American nations were to be aided in seeking escape from old economic practices at home that long had enslaved them.

One of their first visits of state brought the President and Mrs. Kennedy to London, where they were received by Queen Elizabeth and Prince Philip of Great Britain.

Congress adjourned in September. Much of what Kennedy had wanted he gained, but his major rebuffs — Federal aid to schools and medical care for the aged — gave his critics a chance to say that Kennedy lacked courage in risking his personal popularity for the domestic programs in which he professed to believe.

It is easier to criticize a President than to be one, a fact that perhaps even Kennedy did not realize until he assumed office. As a big, restless country, growing in population every hour, the United States never ceases to provide its own problems, its own emergencies.

Surely, in the field of civil rights, Kennedy was forced to come face to face with this reality. Eight years now had passed since the Supreme Court had ruled that public school segregation was unconstitutional, and, understandably, in many areas Negroes were losing patience with the slow pace at which they were gaining this right of equal citizenship.

Progress in integration in schools in Atlanta, Dallas, and Memphis gave some encouragement, but a great deal still remained to be done. 1961 was the year of the "Freedom Riders," who challenged segregation in interstate travel facilities in places like Birmingham and Montgomery, Alabama. Violence resulted and the Kennedy Administration, standing firm by constitutional guarantees, sent United States marshals to the latter city.

Sit-ins, boycotts, picketing, in places as widely separated as Oklahoma City and Norfolk, Virginia, protesting segregation in eating facilities, emphasized the growing dimensions of this problem which also involved practices in housing, in employment, in voting.

Almost inch by inch, John F. Ken-

Above, one of the more relaxed moments in the life of our President. He throws the first ball of the baseball season during the opening game between the Washington Senators and the Baltimore Orioles. In the picture at right, he is shown with 12 selected scouts from all parts of the U.S.A., who present him with a "Report to the Nation."

The First Lady, who speaks fluent French, Spanish, and Italian, accompanies the President during his official visit to Paris to confer with President De Gaulle of France. The visitors from America are greeted at the Elysée Palace by President and Mrs. De Gaulle. (From left to right: Mrs. Gavin, wife of the U.S. Ambassador to France, Mrs. De Gaulle, President Kennedy, President De Gaulle, Mrs. Kennedy, and Mrs. Debre, wife of the French Prime Minister.)

nedy was learning the size of his new job. There was no rest, there was no ease. Yet his smile never wavered. He was willing to learn, willing to grow. In November, he granted to *Izvestia,* the Soviet newspaper, an interview on the basis that it must be published as recorded, and really for the first time the Russian people were given an opportunity of reading what a United States President believed about the great problems facing the world.

Earlier, lifting a shovel of earth in a tree-planting ceremony in Canada, the President aggravated his old back injury, but as the year ended this disability seemed on the mend. During the early summer, he had walked on crutches, but now these were discarded. Then, just before Christmas, his father suffered a stroke and the President and his family spent the holidays at Palm Beach, Florida.

People hoped, for the President's sake, that Papa Joe would recover. America liked Kennedy for his youth-fulness, his small children, his wife, who at official occasions could speak in French and Spanish, his mistakes, his sense of optimism that the free world would survive as he and his fellow naval men had survived years ago in Blackett Strait.

Khrushchev, Castro, civil rights — indeed, the problems of the free world piled up on every side — and yet a feeling persisted, at this first Yuletide season under the Presidency of John F. Kennedy, that somehow the world might stumble forward to "peace on earth, good will toward men."

**When did America enter the Space Age?**

President Kennedy, beginning his second year in office, faced opposition at home and abroad. Congress convened that January with an old foe from Massachusetts, John McCormick, now Speaker of the House, yet McCormick was loyal in support of Kennedy's policies.

At home, the President was accused of being "soft" on Communism, even to the extent of muzzling free speech among his military officers. The obligation to resume the testing of nuclear bombs was a hard decision forced on him by Soviet action, and a new series of United States bomb tests began over Christmas Island in the central Pacific late in April.

But those winter months of 1962 also saw Americans thrilling to a new adventure. President Kennedy participated in the activities when at Cape Canaveral, Florida, at 9:47 a.m., Eastern standard time, on February 20th, Astronaut John H. Glenn, Jr. became the first United States citizen launched into outer space.

Millions of Americans sat breathlessly beside their television sets or radios that morning, waiting for the fateful countdown: "five . . . four . . . three . . . two . . . one." On their television screens, they watched the columns of vapor rising from the base of the rocket that would send Glenn's spaceship, *Friendship 7*, hurtling into an unknown world.

Slowly, the craft lifted skyward, leaving behind a trail of fire. Soon the *Friendship 7* was lost from sight, and few Americans were able to think of anything other than this brave astronaut hurtling around the earth at more than 17,000 miles an hour.

Glenn saw night turn into day, telling praying countrymen: "It's a beautiful sight." Glenn's orbit sometimes carried him as high as 160 miles above the earth, yet passing over our continent he could recognize an irrigated desert, a

bridge, the Gulf Stream. Three orbits were completed in about 4 hours 56 minutes before Glenn parachuted to safety some 166 miles east of Grand Turk Island in the Bahamas.

In late May, a second astronaut, H. Scott Carpenter, also completed three orbits and in early October Astronaut Walter M. Schirra, Jr., completed six orbits. That, under Kennedy, America had taken its place as an unfailing pioneer of the Space Age was, of course, an unforgettable achievement of his years in the White House.

But such success could only be measured by the problems that never end for the President. Laos and neighboring Thailand both were scenes of renewed Communist aggression in 1962, yet Kennedy did not flinch; he sent marines and soldiers into Thailand until, at Geneva, an agreement was signed guaranteeing that Laos should be a neutral and independent nation. Meanwhile, Mexico greeted President and Mrs. Kennedy with warmth and affection during a three-day visit in June.

Already a spectacular success by the fall of the year was the Peace Corps,

Like millions of other Americans, President and Mrs. Kennedy watch the take-off and flight of our astronauts on their TV set in the White House.

President Kennedy presents the NASA Distinguished Service Award to Astronaut John Glenn in February, 1962.

established by an executive order of the President on March 1, 1961. Under the leadership of Robert Sargent Shriver, Jr., a Chicago businessman and Mr. Kennedy's brother-in-law, the Peace Corps enlisted Americans of all ages into a volunteer movement to help underdeveloped nations through programs of education.

Pay was small in the Peace Corps, the opportunity for human service enormous, and by the end of 1962 almost 3,500 Americans served in 38 countries, while more than 900 were in training for future service. As teachers, farm specialists, nurses, engineers, bricklayers, carpenters, surveyors, among other callings, the members of the Peace Corps won friends for America around the world.

Hospital teams worked in Malaysia. Other volunteers ran summer camps for underprivileged children in the Philippines. Farmers on Cyprus were taught the latest scientific advances in raising chickens. The toil of the Peace Corps went on around the clock. The range of its activities seemed to have no limit.

September brought a frightful crisis arising from a Federal Court order that James H. Meredith, a Negro Air Force veteran, must be admitted as a student to the all-white University of Mississippi. In this Deep South state, once the home of the president of the Confederacy, segregationist sentiment ruled the state's politics. When, accompanied by officials of the United States Department of Justice, Meredith applied for admission to the University, his path was barred by Mississippi's Governor Ross R. Barnett.

On a second attempt, Barnett once more prevented Meredith from enroll-

**What was the crisis in Oxford?**

41

ing and a day later the Negro was again rejected by Lieutenant Governor Paul Johnson, who was supported by the state police. Next day, learning that state police and an angry crowd had gathered at the entrance to the University, Meredith and his Federal guards did not try to gain admission. The United States Fifth District Court, finding the Governor guilty of civil contempt, ordered him to admit Meredith as a student by October 2nd or face arrest and heavy fines.

Sickly, the rest of the nation watched the crisis grow. Hundreds of Federal deputy marshals were sent to Oxford, the site of the University of Mississippi. Troops were alerted to stand by, should the situation worsen, and President Kennedy federalized the Mississippi National Guard.

The Governor remained defiant and a spirit of rebellion, unequalled since Civil War days, hung over Oxford when on the last day of September a contingent of Federal marshals brought Meredith to the campus. In a nationwide television broadcast, President Kennedy appealed to Barnett and citizens of Mississippi to obey the orders of the Court.

The plea came too late. Days of crying that, if necessary, Mississippi would stand alone among the 50 states in resisting desegregation had whipped irresponsible elements into a frenzy.

Rioting broke out on the campus. Students, joined by adult Mississippians and rabid segregationists who had come from out of state, attacked the Federal marshals. Cars were turned over and burned, windows smashed. Shots rang out, killing two men (one was a French newspaper reporter). Hundreds were injured. The assaults lasted for hours and were ended only after the arrival of troops and the use of tear gas.

With the marshals still present, Meredith finally was allowed to attend classes at the University in subsequent days.

The Meredith case simply emphasized the fact that civil rights no longer was a national issue that could be brushed aside with vague promises of a remedy some time in an uncertain future. Mass demonstrations against segregation in lunchrooms, movie theaters, and waiting rooms led to many arrests in Albany, Georgia. In Mississippi and Georgia, churches were burned after Negroes gathered there to receive instruction in how to register as voters. Thus the tensions heightened — upon America, upon the young man in the White House.

Shocked though the people were by rioting and death **How did America come to the brink of war?** in Oxford, Mississippi, a much graver peril soon confronted the nation. In late October when Kennedy canceled a speech in Chicago and returned to Washington, the official explanation was that the President had a cold. Soon, other persons important in the national Government were hurrying to the White House.

In a calm, firm voice, President Kennedy addressed the nation over television on October 22nd, revealing that the Government had learned beyond doubt of the existence of ballistic mis-

This now-famous picture shows the President in his office clapping hands while Caroline and "John-John" dance.

sile bases on Cuba which were being constructed with assistance from the Soviet Union. The strike capacity of these missiles would be such, the President said, that they would threaten most of the North American continent and could reach as far south as Lima, Peru. Until these bases were dismantled and the flow of offensive weapons to Cuba stopped, he added, the United States would impose a quarantine (or blockade) upon the island.

Somberly, the President said: "It shall be the policy of this nation to regard any nuclear missile launched from Cuba against any nation in the Western Hemisphere as an attack by the Soviet Union on the United States requiring a full retaliatory response on the Soviet Union."

The country, bracing for the possibility of a nuclear war, was quiet, tense, prepared to stand by the President. The nations of South America and Great Britain stood firmly behind Kennedy's policy. A report that 25 Russian ships were approaching Cuba heightened the tension. Would they turn back? If not, would we sink them?

With the knowledge that the start of World War III could hinge upon the answers to these two questions, United Nations Secretary U Thant worked to avoid a conflict. Messages were exchanged between the President and Premier Khrushchev. On October 28th, Moscow issued the order to dismantle the rocket bases and return the missiles to Russia. The President hailed Khrushchev's "statesmanlike decision."

As the year ended, it was clear that John F. Kennedy had grown in stature.

He had the backbone to stand up to Khrushchev, people said, and the whole world was better for that fact. A popular photograph of the President showed him in his office, clapping hands, while Caroline and her young brother John, Jr., danced. Americans smiled in a warm-hearted way. They liked thinking of their young President as a family man.

President Kennedy began his third year

**Why did Kennedy become a world hero?** in the White House as a leader who gave hope to the world that more peaceful times lay ahead. True, as far as the cold war with the Soviets was concerned, areas of deep unrest remained and others would soon develop. Russian troops and technicians, still stationed in Cuba, troubled many Americans. When United States military convoys, en route to Berlin, were delayed at Soviet checkpoints, the action scarcely promoted friendly negotiations. And we became involved against Communist guerrillas in South Vietnam, where we stood firm for the right of the smaller nations of Southeast Asia to choose their own governments.

Yet despite these points of stress, the feeling continued that even Khrushchev looked with growing respect upon Kennedy as a force in the world and that, therefore, prospects for future harmony between the East and West had brightened.

This montage shows the President alone and thoughtful, surrounded by problems on which he must make the final decisions. The sign saying "The buck stops here" was kept by President Truman on his desk as a constant reminder that the ultimate responsibility is the President's.

Indeed, Kennedy called boldly for a new approach to the problems dividing the great power-blocs. New hope, new thinking, new action — this was the sum of Kennedy's appeal, his formula for leadership in international affairs —and Khrushchev responded cordially to his overtures. That summer, the signing of a limited nuclear test-ban treaty by the United States, the United Kingdom, and the Soviet Union was hailed as a first step toward that more secure future for which so many people yearned.

When Kennedy visited West Germany and Ireland, hundreds of thousands of Europeans cheered the President. No one knew better than they that a positive peace had not yet

From a specially-built platform at the Brandenburg Gate, President Kennedy gazes over the wall dividing East and West Berlin. During his visit June 26, 1963, thousands of Berliners and West Germans wildly cheered the speech of the courageous world leader.

been achieved, but John F. Kennedy — young, strong, and confident — was their symbol of faith in the years ahead.

At home, the President lived with the serious reality of the "Negro revolt," in America the most significant series of events in 1963. The trouble began in Birmingham, the largest city in Alabama and long known to Negroes as "the capital of segregation." Under the leadership of the Reverend Martin Luther King, Jr., president of the Southern Christian Leadership Conference, and the Reverend Fred L. Shuttlesworth, president of the Alabama Christian Movement for Human Rights, fellow Negroes staged demonstrations for the rights guaranteed them under existing Federal laws.

**What was the revolt of 1963?**

Eugene Connor, Commissioner of Public Safety in Birmingham and a champion of segregation, led a violent reaction. Police dogs were turned on demonstrators. Heavy fire hoses swept them from the streets. Children were treated as ruthlessly as adults, and the spectacle of this merciless treatment, revealed by television cameras, sickened the nation. By early May, more than 1,000 demonstrators (at least half Negroes under the age of 18) had been jailed.

President Kennedy intervened, believing that he had secured a truce by which both sides could negotiate sensibly. Three days later, the home of a leader of the Negro demonstrators was bombed, setting off worse riots.

A crowd of better than 2,500 Negroes attacked the police. Bricks and bottles flew through the air. Cars were overturned and burned. Six small stores and a two-story apartment house were demolished. Fifty persons were injured. President Kennedy stationed Federal troops near Birmingham, and, gradually, the tensions eased.

Thus began the pattern of the "Negro revolt" of 1963, the most militant uprising in America since the days of

45

the Civil War. American hearts were chilled by such incidents as these:

— The bombing of a Negro Baptist Church in Birmingham, where four girls were killed and several children, attending Sunday School, were injured.

— The shooting to death of a white civil rights crusader, walking from Tennessee to Mississippi, on a roadside near Attalla, Alabama.

— The shooting in the back of Medgar Evers, a leader of the National Association of Colored People in Jackson, the capital of Mississippi.

The North, no less than the South, was showing increasing resistance to Negro demands for full citizenship and in the White House, Kennedy faced a problem no President had known since the time of Abraham Lincoln. These two men, the 16th and 35th Presidents of the United States, both had approached the problem of the Negro from the same basis, hoping that time and education and moderation would solve the racial and human problems involved. Both had realized that only the public interest invested within the Federal Government could combat the private interests invested within state governments. Both grew older, wiser, more abused because they recognized this struggle.

Lincoln, within his lifetime — before he was assassinated — took the first step, freeing the Negroes as slaves and giving them the chance to grow up to full citizenship. Now, after a century, John F. Kennedy realized that he also must face facts, no matter what the decision might cost him in terms of his political future.

In this spirit, on June 19, 1963, the President addressed a special message to Congress. Birmingham's tragedy, he said, should have taught the nation that the "result of continued Federal legislative inaction" would not only "continue" but "increase" racial strife. He submitted to Congress proposals on civil rights in three areas:

1. In facilities related to interstate commerce — hotels, restaurants, stores — where all citizens should be guaranteed equal rights;

2. When citizens were denied their civil rights — especially in cases of school desegregation — the United States District Attorney should be empowered to bring suit on behalf of these legally injured individuals; and

3. Racial discrimination on work supported by Federal funds should be outlawed and, where necessary, other Federal funds should provide vocational training for Negroes until they were qualified to hold such jobs.

Not since Lincoln had any President struck so hard, or at greater political risk, for the equality of all Americans. Not at the typewriter, but in his rocking chair at the White House, John F. Kennedy was adding a new chapter to his *Profiles in Courage*.

At home, however, the news was not all gloomy. On May 25, 1961, in a message to Congress, President Kennedy had said: "I believe this nation should commit itself to achieving the goal, before this decade is out, of landing a man on the moon and returning him safely to earth." Critics of the President, estimating that the cost of such a project would run to

**What heritage did he give America?**

at least $40 billion had ridiculed him as an impossible dreamer.

Then in 1962, Astronauts Glenn, Schirra, and Carpenter had completed successful orbits in outer space, and the dream had not seemed so impossible. And on May 15, 1963, Americans again sat fascinated before television screens as they watched L. Gordon Cooper, Jr., in his spaceship, *Faith 7,* blasted off the launching pad at Cape Canaveral. For 22 times, before returning safely to earth, Cooper "orbited" the globe.

And so in 1963, the image of John F. Kennedy grew — as our first statesman of the Space Age, as the symbol of hope for securing peace in a troubled world, as the champion of equal rights for all citizens without regard to the color of their skins.

Understandably, Americans were saddened when they learned that another son, Patrick Bouvier Kennedy, born on August 7, 1963, had died two days later. They were glad to see Mrs. Kennedy recover, and with satisfaction they watched her, radiantly happy beside her husband, receiving a bouquet of roses at the Dallas airport on that fateful 22nd of November. Not long afterward, an assassin's bullet ended the life of the 35th President of the United States.

All of America seemed to share the same great heartbreak. They had watched this young man growing — indeed, in hope, in new vision, within themselves, sometimes knowingly, sometimes unknowingly, they had been growing with him. Now — unexpectedly, unjustly, cruelly — he was dead. The fact was without sense.

So only the grief of the people endured — in America, around the world.

Numbed, Americans watched on television as Lyndon B. Johnson was sworn into office as the 36th President of the United States, and their hearts reached out to embrace this tall Texan, who was thrust so suddenly into the greatest responsibility on earth.

Stunned by the unbelievable fact that the young President is dead, victim of a senseless assassination, Lyndon B. Johnson is sworn in as President of the United States of America in the cabin of the Presidential plane as Mrs. Jacqueline Kennedy stands at his side. (Mrs. Johnson is at his right in the background.) Judge Sarah T. Hughes administers the oath of office.

But their real love was for Jacqueline B. Kennedy, for young Caroline, for little "John-John," who, brave in their sorrow, gave to every American a sense of dignity in the knowledge that the First Lady and the children of the fallen President were worthy heirs of his trust.

The body of the President lay in the East Room of the White House on November 23rd and next day a horse-drawn caisson carried his flag-draped casket to the rotunda of the Capitol. All day, all night, grieving Americans waited — close to 250,000 in number — to pay their last respects to the young man who had once been second-best in his family and was now the first citizen of the world.

When on November 25th the casket, followed by a riderless black horse, was led to the funeral and burial, 92 nations were represented in the solemn procession. Through tear-dimmed eyes, watching on television, Americans recognized many of the greatest leaders of the world: the President of France, the Emperor of Ethiopia, Prince Philip of Great Britain, the Queen of Greece, the King of Belgium, the Crown Princess and Prince of the Netherlands, the President of Ireland, the Mayor of West Berlin, the Premier of Japan, the President of South Korea, among others.

On a restful hillside in Arlington National Cemetery, across the quiet Potomac from the White House and the Lincoln Memorial, the body of John F. Kennedy was laid to rest. Within a few hours, Americans formed lines, waiting patiently to visit this peaceful graveside. They came next day and the next and the next — they came week after week, month after month, in good weather and bad — and in little more than half a year more than 3,000,000 Americans paid their last respects to Mr. Kennedy. Some brought flowers. Some prayed. Almost all wept.

Why?

No one knew better than the President who no longer lived. In the spring of 1963, he had said:

". . . We all inhabit this small planet. We all breathe the same air. We all cherish our children's future."

But to work for peace and one's fellow men, to dare to brave any tempest that appeared — ah, that was what freedom and the American dream were all about — and *that* was the heritage to America of John F. Kennedy.

Mrs. John F. Kennedy, Caroline, and John, Jr., kneel at the grave of the late President in Arlington National Cemetery. They lay flowers near the eternal light on the 47th anniversary of Mr. Kennedy's birth.